IMAGES
of England

AROUND
COUNTESTHORPE

The only surviving box-framed house in Countesthorpe is 5 Main Street. Deeds survive from 1618 showing ownership by John Gillam who leased it to Clement Clarke. It was originally one property but had been converted into three cottages by the middle of the nineteenth century. This picture was taken just after the turn of the twentieth century. Standing in the doorway is William Henry Hubbard, one of the local butchers and graziers, and on the right is William Barlow, the village's last resident blacksmith and farrier.

IMAGES
of England

AROUND
COUNTESTHORPE

Compiled by
Henrietta Schultka and Ann True

TEMPUS

First published 1999
Copyright © Henrietta Schultka and Ann True, 1999

Tempus Publishing Limited
The Mill, Brimscombe Port,
Stroud, Gloucestershire, GL5 2QG

ISBN 0 7524 1556 5

Typesetting and origination by
Tempus Publishing Limited
Printed in Great Britain by
Midway Clark Printing, Wiltshire

A VE Day street party in Main Street, 1945, that was supervised by Mrs Mason, Mrs Taylor,
Mrs Marion Briggs and her daughter-in-law, Ada Briggs.

Contents

Acknowledgements

Many of the photographs included in this book are part of Henrietta Schultka's personal collection, some of which she has taken herself. We would like to thank all those who generously donated additional photographs, including those we were unable to feature in this edition. Acknowledgements are also due to Peter Elliott, the Leicestershire Record Office at Long Street, Wigston Magna and the Leicester *Mercury*. We wish to make particular mention of the valuable assistance given by Ian Patterson.

Books consulted include *History of the County of Leicestershire* by John Nichols and G.F. Farnham's *Leicestershire Medieval Village Notes*. Both books can be located at the Leicestershire Record Office.

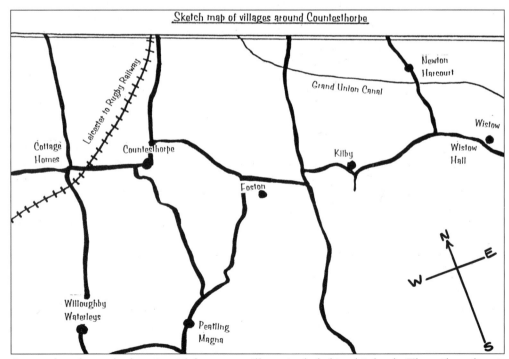

A map that shows the location of the seven villages included in this book. The railway line is now disused, but its position can still clearly be seen.

Introduction

Although they are situated within a radius of four miles, the seven villages featured in this book display significant differences in their development. These differences were dependent on whether the village was 'open' or 'closed', whether religious conformity was accepted or challenged and at what stage in its development it was affected by enclosure. 'Open' villages did not have a dominant landowner; the land was shared amongst numerous small landowners. 'Closed' villages were dominated by one or a small number of landowners.

As an open village, Countesthorpe's culture was diverse and religious nonconformity was tolerated. It was essentially an agricultural village, the daughter settlement of Blaby. The name 'Countesthorpe' means a farm settlement in the field, possibly once held by a countess. The village was first mentioned in records in 1209 as 'Le Thorp' and by 1276 it was named 'Thorp Cuntasse'.

Once the village had become self-sufficient, with its farmers, miller, carpenter and blacksmith for example, the lifestyle of the villagers became established. Houses were confined to the centre of the settlement as agricultural land was valuable. The parish comprised a number of very large open fields that were divided into strips. Villagers grew their crops in these fields and also had a share of meadow ground and common pasture for their stock. There were numerous small landowners. Local families included the Gillams, Lords, Johnsons, Gumleys, Burleys, Carrs, Elliotts and Heathcotes.

Enclosure of the open fields began in 1767 leading to the landscape becoming completely altered and the lifestyle of many of the villagers changing. It had been suggested that enclosure would improve farming techniques and create greater productivity. In effect, it ended the long period of co-operative farming that Countesthorpe had enjoyed and replaced it with competitive farming. Where unemployment resulted, the manufacture of socks and stockings offered an initial solution.

Evidence of developing trade and industry in Countesthorpe is contained in the 1801 census. Framework knitting began at the beginning of the eighteenth century and, by 1801, 310 people were shown as being engaged in trade or manufacture out of a total population of 540.

The spirit of non-conformity became apparent with the setting up of the Baptist Sunday School in 1792 and the registration of George Beale's dwelling house for divine worship in 1794. In addition, the Primitive Methodist group was founded in the village in the early nineteenth century. The existence of various public houses also contributed to the character of Countesthorpe as an open village.

Willoughby Waterleys was essentially a small agricultural village, consisting of one street with farms on either side. The original medieval village appears to have been located around the church. Its name ('Wilebi' in 1086) means 'among the willows' and reflects the springs and rivulets which are a feature of the parish.

Willoughby was a closed village, its manorial rights moving from family to family. In the Middle Ages the land was owned by the Norman family of de Angerville, but in 1347 Richard Angerville, the last of that family to be mentioned in Willoughby, took holy orders and forsook his family name. The manorial rights were then passed on to the Astleys of Broughton Astley and the Grey family, through Lady Jane Grey's grandfather. They were eventually sold to Mrs Blucke whose son, Revd W.S. Blucke, was the inhabitant from 1858-1898.

In 1729 the parish of Willoughby was united with Peatling Magna, one of the oldest settlements in Leicestershire. It is shown as 'Petlinge' in the *Domesday Book* and this means 'settlement on rising ground of Poetla's people'. It is believed that the medieval village was spread over a slightly different area than the position it has today. The Jervis family were lords of the manor for around 200 years from Elizabethan times. Several of their tombs can be seen in the twelfth-century church.

Like Willoughby Waterleys in 1637, Peatling Magna was also enclosed privately in the seventeenth century, a practice that was possible because it was a closed village. Foston, another village that was enclosed privately around the same time, suffered a different fate. Originally called 'Fot's tun', an old Scandinavian personal name, Foston is situated seven miles south-east from Leicester. According to Farnham's Leicestershire *Medieval Village Notes*, 'There is land for five ploughs. In demesne there are two ploughs; and two serfs and one bondwoman; and eleven sochmen with eight villeins and four bordars have five ploughs. There are sixteen acres of meadow.'

The lay subsidy of 1327 showed thirteen men and one woman eligible to pay the poll tax levied in that year. In 1564 there were twenty families living in the village. Towards the end of the reign of Henry VIII, William Faunt, a lawyer of the Inner Temple and of Wistow in Huntingdon, bought the manor of Foston. It was a closed parish with only one freeholder, no non-conformity and no dissenters. Faunt's descendants were responsible for the enclosure of Foston for the grazing of sheep. This was completed by 1636, except for the 100 acres of glebe. The lay subsidy of 1571 showed that only two men paid the tax. In 1666, the Hearth Tax showed Colonel Faunt had thirteen hearths at Foston Hall, Mr Thomas Mawson had four, the Parsonage House had three, and Robert Staine and Francis Simson had one each. It is difficult to assess the number of people living in Foston by these figures as poor people did not pay the hearth tax, but it is thought that the depopulation of Foston began with William Faunt.

Like Foston, the village of Kilby was mentioned in the *Domesday Book*. The old village was situated round the church that now stands isolated about a quarter of a mile from the village. The name 'Kilby' means 'of the children' (i.e. retainers) and was written as 'Cilebi' in 1086.

Kilby was a hamlet of the parish of Wistow and consisted of twelve ploughlands. It was freely held by Eur during the reign of Edward the Confessor and was worth forty shillings. The value was the same in the Norman Survey when it was held by Oger the Briton. There were twelve acres of meadow and a mill valued at two shillings.

Together with Newton Harcourt, Kilby was enclosed in 1771. Kilby contained around 1,020 acres of open fields, meadows, common pastures and wasteland, and Newton Harcourt contained 1,100. Sir Charles Halford was lord of the manors of Kilby and Newton, and patron of Wistow.

Newton Harcourt, a daughter settlement of Wistow, was held by Richard Harcourt around 1240. Originally held by Aeilric, a freeman, son of Meriet, during the reign of Edward the Confessor, it was later given to Richard in marriage with Arabell, daughter of the Earl of Winchester. In the Itinerary of 1280, Newton, Wistow, Fleckeneye and Sadinton answered collectively as one village. Divided by the Grand Union Canal, Newton Harcourt consisted of the chapel and one large house on the south side, and the rest of the village on the north side.

Wistow, meaning stow or holy place, was in possession of the D'Halfords and the Hastings family during the Middle Ages. In 1603 it was bought by Andrew Halford, a descendant of the earlier D'Halfords.

During the late sixteenth and early seventeenth centuries, there are references to the land around the church of St Wistan's being flooded. In 1775 records show that the lordship of Wistow was an old enclosure and contained 892 acres. Sheep were grazed but there were only two houses, the Hall and a shepherd's house. The village of Wistow became deserted but Wistow Hall remains.

Ann True

One

Countesthorpe

This picture showing the north end of Main Street and The Square was taken in 1906. On the left is the National School, in the centre is Seaton's farmhouse and on the right the three-storey building is the King William IV Inn. The National School was built in 1843 on land that was purchased by Revd Edward Stokes for ten shillings in 1753. Before giving it to the parish, he erected a building, the upper floor of which was to be used as both a school and parish offices. According to the school deeds drawn up in April 1753, the schoolchildren were to be taught to 'read, write and cost up Accounts ... and for the Parish Officers of Countesthorpe aforesaid to meet and transact their Business in relating to the said Parish.' The ground floor consisted of a parlour, stables, two coalhouses and two necessary houses.

This postcard was sent by a village resident in 1911 at a cost of 1/2d. The view of Main Street, taken from The Square, shows the Leicester Co-op on the left, and the single storey building is the smithy. This is possibly the only pictorial record of the blacksmith's shop, run by the Barlow family for around eighty years. Miss Florence Brett and Mrs Ann Moore (née Burley) can be seen in the front garden of the corner house.

This interior of a typical late-Victorian living room shows Mrs Ann Moore, with a cat on her knee, sitting by the fireside with her friend, Mrs Page. Her home was situated on the corner of Church Street and Main Street. Of particular interest are the family photographs and china ornaments on the wall and mantelpiece, the spice cupboards either side of the fire and the pegged rag rug on the floor, which make a comfortable picture of the times. Ann's husband was a local carpenter and they had no children.

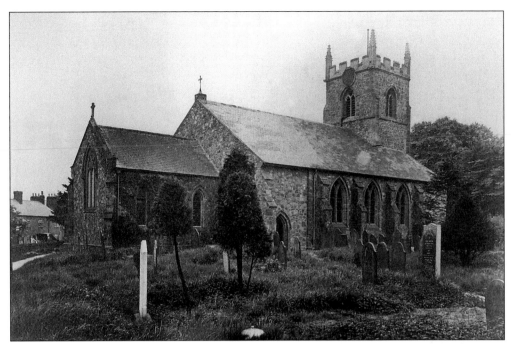

St Andrew's Church showing the alterations that were made by the Chapman Brothers in 1907. The chancel was shortened and the nave lengthened to increase its seating capacity. The churchyard was later cleared and the tombstones moved around the church boundary.

This fancy dress photograph, c. 1930, is significant for its original Countesthorpe Conservative Club sign. Pictured, from left to right: Fred Findley, Arthur Lucas and Ernest Riddington.

Situated on the left of this photograph of Main Street is the house known as 'The Elms'. The vicar of St Andrew's Church lived here until the vicarage on Station Road was built. In the 1891 census, the Revd Matthew Henry Boden was recorded as living here with his wife, Jane, seven children and a servant.

This view of the Roebuck Inn, taken in 1906, illustrates the shuttered windows and the header and stretcher brickwork. The last landlord of the Roebuck was Andrew Swanwick. In 1926 the building became a private house. It was demolished, together with neighbouring properties, between 1961 and 1962 to make way for the Conservative Club car park and Scout Hut.

'Little Questing', situated on Peatling Road, is the only surviving building in Countesthorpe with mud walls up to the first level. The upper storey is made of brick. Nothing was built on this land before enclosure in 1767, but census reports show that John Chapman, a bricklayer, and his wife Sabina lived in a house there in 1841. By 1881 it was still occupied by their descendants, Thomas and Ruth Chapman.

Austrey Lane was formerly one of the roads from Leicester to Lutterworth. After enclosure it was also designated as a bridleway and footpath to Peatling Magna and Willoughby. The road takes its name from Austrey in Warwickshire from where the Monk's Charity, set up through Thomas Monk's will in 1713, was administered. Thomas Monk is believed to have had family connections with Countesthorpe, and the rent from land which he owned was used to fund the apprenticeship of seven poor boys in Austrey, Measham, Shenton and Whitwick. The ladies in the picture, taken around 1920, are Miss Wale on the far left, and Margaret Weston and her children, Mary and Marjorie, on the right. The house that stood on this site, which was purchased by John Grant from Francis Estley of Broughton Astley in 1670, was thatched and timber-framed. In 1740 it was rebuilt with brick by the Grants. By 1851 it was divided into the three cottages shown.

Members of the Page family stand outside Home Farm on Main Street. All that remains of the original farmhouse is the right-hand section. Around 1930 the rest was demolished and a new building erected which faced north instead of west.

When this picture was taken, in about 1932, the scene had remained unchanged for around 180 years, with the exception of the war memorial and style of transport. All that remains today is the timbered house and the barn on the left.

This view, looking north-west, shows the wall surrounding the school yard, on what was known as Penfold Corner. Pictured in the centre are two cottages that were built in the eighteenth century and have now been demolished. On the right is a large farmhouse that later became a post office. It became the home of Dr Wynn Barnley in the late 1920s.

This photograph was taken on 24 November 1921, after the unveiling of the war memorial by the Duke of York, and shows the original King William IV Inn that had been built as a farmhouse in 1751. It was demolished in August 1939 when John Mee was the landlord. The new public house was built on the land behind the inn prior to its demolition.

This section of the road is now called Wigston Street. The picture was taken around 1910 and shows the shop on the corner of Green Lane which was opened in the late nineteenth century by a member of the Immins family. The business was taken over in 1926 by Ernest and Clarice Heathcote. It was a typical general store selling many items including food, stamps, postcards, cigarettes, tobacco, snuff and haberdashery goods. Clarice continued to run the business after her husband's death in 1969 until she retired at the age of ninety-four in November 1993. After the shop closed, it was converted back to residential use.

Seen here around 1931 are Hunt's Garage and Beaconsfield Terrace on Leicester Road. Herbert Hunt was a carrier and he also had a landau which was used for weddings. The petrol pumps were the first seen in Countesthorpe. From the end of May 1998 the sale of petrol ceased from these premises. The boy with the bicycle is Alan Higgs.

These two pictures show the destruction of the houses on the north side of Brook Street. It made way for the development of sheltered accommodation for the elderly known as Brook Court.

This is the second Baptist Church which was erected on Church Street in Countesthorpe It was built on land adjoining the first church in 1863. This was also the date when it became independent from the church at Arnesby.

The Baptist Church decorated for a harvest festival during the middle of the 1930s.

The north side of Central Street, taken around 1935. Arthur Lucas can be seen pointing up the gable at the end of the house. The house was owned by John Thomas Barlow, whose father was the last traditional blacksmith in the village. Since 1935 it has been demolished to make way for a car park and public toilets. The builders' cart was used to transport tools and equipment when working in the village.

Liz Johnson and a friend standing outside her house on Hall Lane (now Station Road), in 1911.

This picture of Chapman's house and builder's yard on Station Road, was taken around 1910. The footpath to Whetstone ran beside the house.

The Post Office, Countesthorpe.

This view of a virtually traffic-free Station Road, *c.* 1960, contrasts sharply with its modern equivalent where speeding cars are more prevalent. The post office was formerly situated in Central Street and was run by Mr and Mrs Butcher. When the business transferred to Station Road, it was opened up by Mr and Mrs Fletcher.

A view of Countesthorpe Railway Station, with the second Railway Inn in the background, taken around 1960. The first building was situated in what is now the Hinckley and Rugby Building Society. Within a few years of this photograph being taken, the station, and many other small ones like it, were closed by the Government consultant, Dr Beeching.

An engine shunting a carriage brought to Countesthorpe Station to be stored in the sidings, as the railways were wound down, *c.* 1961. The railway line, which ran from Leicester to Rugby, was opened in 1840 and closed on 1 February 1962.

Families from the Baptist, Methodist and Church of England Sunday schools wait for the train to take them on the last combined outing to Skegness in 1961.

This picture of No. 11 Cottage Home, Countesthorpe, was taken around 1910. The building was demolished to make way for the entrance to Countesthorpe College, which is off Winchester Road.

The centre of the village, *c.* 1965, seen with the newly built Jelson estate in the top right and the beginnings of the Linden Farm estate in the top left. The village population remained static until 1960, but increased significantly after this time.

Two houses on Willoughby Road taken after they suffered bomb damage on the night of Easter Sunday, 1941. The pilot of a stray plane, returning from bombing Coventry, dropped his surplus bombs in an attempt to damage the railway line. He missed his target, but damaged these houses and an allotment called The Hags off Glebe Drive. The house on the right was repaired, but the one on the left had to be demolished soon after as the explosion caused it to move off its foundations.

This aerial view of the junction where Leicester Road and Foston Road meet was taken around 1960. At this time Foston Road School was still in use.

Canal bridge number 92 at Crow Mill on Countesthorpe Road, South Wigston, before it was widened to take modern traffic.

The road to Countesthorpe where it crosses the River Sence at Crow Mill, *c.* 1960. The viaduct was demolished following the closing of the Midland railway line from Leicester to Rugby on 1 January 1962.

Hospital Lane was once part of the turnpike road from Barlestone to Foston. It was also known as the Coalcart Road, as coal was once brought into the area via this road. The road under the railway bridge was often flooded after heavy rain and the bridge was demolished in 1969.

The men and children of the Chapman family building a haystack at the beginning of the twentieth century.

William Mason of Wigston Magna is photographed here in 1908, cutting the corn in a field next to the road to Peatling Magna. This postcard was used as an advertisement.

Arthur Page (far left) and three of his farm labourers, Tom Barron, William John Mawby and Albert Mawby, haymaking around 1929.

William John Mawby was employed by his brother-in-law, John Page, who farmed at Home Farm in Main Street. William is seen here, still working in the harvest field, aged seventy.

Bill Barlow trying his hand at farming with his grandfather, John Mawby, looking on.

Members of the Page, Mawby and Barlow families taking a break from harvesting. They are, from left to right: -?-, Violet Ward (maid to the Page family), Arthur Page, Louisa Barlow, Bill Barlow, Albert Mawby, Tom Barron.

One of the many buses that ran from Countesthorpe in the early 1920s. This bus belonged to the company run by Jim Lewitt (shown in the picture) and his brother Len.

Another bus service that was run by local men. William James Sweet, the owner of this bus, was also the landlord of both the Bull's Head and the Axe and Square public houses in the village.

This picture was taken during the early 1920s and shows the ambulance from the Isolation Hospital, Blaby, which came to collect patients sick with diphtheria and scarlet fever.

Henry Ward, a grazier and carrier, with his horse and wagon at Countesthorpe station in the 1920s.

This lorry, carrying large baskets of hosiery, was owned by Herbert Hunt, a carrier from Leicester Road. On a Wednesday, the lorry would be converted into a bus by adding benches, a frame and a tarpaulin. Fare paying passengers would be taken into Leicester for market day.

A builder's labourer taking his lunch break. John (Jack) Peat a locally born man, worked for both Thirlby and Stretton Builders.

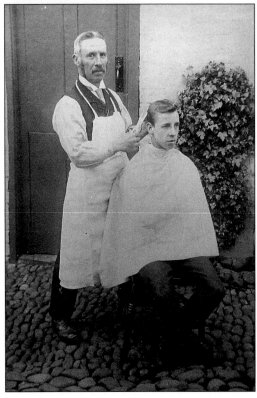

The village barber, Henry Herbert, c. 1910, outside his house in Cox's Lane (now Central Street) demonstrating his hairdressing skills on one of his sons.

Herbert Clarke, a local farmer, was also the night soil man and dustman. His horse and cart are parked in Central Street, *c.* 1929. The boy is Bill Barlow.

Local dustmen and woman employed by Blaby Rural District Council, around 1950. Arthur Hubbard and John William Barlow are on the far right.

Frank Lucas, seen here serving a customer, was probably the longest serving landlord at The Bull's Head from 1936-1961. This photograph was taken shortly before his death.

The Fleckney butcher serving customers on Cosby Road, c. 1941. The butcher is Ronny Capel and next to him are, from left to right: Mr Skeffington, -?-, Mrs Tompkin, Joan Tompkin. Joan has just come from Countesthorpe railway station. She was taking her last leave before being posted abroad for the duration of the war.

John Burley, a Methodist preacher, was born in 1822 and died in 1910. He was the second son of John Burley and Elizabeth March. He married Elizabeth Haywood and they had one daughter, Eliza Ann.

Henry and Suzanna Blake, members of the Society of Friends (Quakers), on 5 November 1957. Notice the lack of lapels on the man's jacket, and the lady's bonnet.

The Revd Samuel H. Tomes, the vicar of Countesthorpe for forty years, seen here with five members of the choir, all from the Chapman family.

This picture of PC Spibey, Countesthorpe's local policeman, was taken during the 1920s.

Nurse Conway was the local district nurse and midwife. By 1930 she had left the village and was working at Bond Street Maternity Hospital in Leicester.

Dr E. Wynne Barnley established a practice in the village during 1925, with the help of Dr Ruth Brittan. This was almost unique as there were only around 1,000 female GPs in the whole country. She retired in 1962 and died shortly afterwards. The road, Barnley Close, was named after her and a plaque was fixed to the Rainbow Shop in memory of her contribution to the local community over many years.

Members of the Parish Council making a presentation to an unknown lady, *c.* 1970. Around the table are, from left to right: Mrs Edith Findley, Percy Lord, Stan Cheney, Mr Noel the parish clerk, -?-, Dr Hoffler the chairman, Bill Riddington, Arthur Cosby, John Winterton, Mr Duffield.

Lily Dalby and her sister, Ivy, cooling their feet in Foston Brook, *c.* 1928.

Countesthorpe schoolchildren in around 1880. The man in the top hat is the headmaster and the little girl by his knee is his daughter. The family lived on Austrey Lane.

Countesthorpe Church of England School pupils during 1914. Holding the board is Beatrice Garratt, and on her left are Renee Stocker and Dolly Johnson. Second from the left on the middle row is Ivy Turner and on her left is Maggie Chapman.

Mr Shuttlewood and a group of enthusiastic gardeners at school, c. 1932. Wilf Mould is holding the hoe on the left and next to him are: Eric Hewitt, Eddie Neal, -?-, Ray Findley, -?-, Jack Clarkmead, Cyril Cosby and Albert Burford dressed in Scout uniform. Owen Thornton is sitting in the front left, holding the spade, with Dennis Warner. Ron Linnett is sitting on the extreme right and standing third from the right is Ron Lane.

Arthur L. Briggs took over temporary charge of Foston School on 31 January 1916, becoming a permanent member of staff on 1 March. He volunteered for army service in the First World War returned to school duties on 17 February 1919. He finally left on 25 March 1921, moving to teach at Enderby. He died in 1965 aged seventy-six.

Foston Road Council School, 1935. Mr Ellingworth presents the school with a scrap album. Any pictures or newspaper cuttings that the children brought in were stuck in the album.

Brown Owl (Mrs Leacroft) and Tawny Owl (Hilary Smart) with their Brownie pack during the early 1950s.

Villagers in fancy dress standing outside the Axe and Square public house on Whit Monday, c. 1924. According to the Alehouse Records that began in 1753 the first licence application for the premises known as the Axe and Square came from John Bent in 1782. It can be surmised that, as the Bent family who originally built the property were carpenters, the sign of the public house relates to their trade. The children in the band came from the Countesthorpe Cottage Homes.

Workers from Tompkins' hosiery factory taking part in the procession of floats for the Whit Monday Infirmary Fête, c. 1934. Pictured are, from left to right: Gladys Cobley, Nellie Wilford, Jinny Hubbard, Maud Weston, Hilda Herbert.

Edward Flude, the son of Ephraim and Elizabeth Flude (née Stevens), was born at Foston. In the 1891 census he is entered as being aged eight and living at Kilby Bridge with his parents. He spent his adult life in Countesthorpe.

One of the forty-seven soldiers from Countesthorpe who died in World War One. Private Sidney Weston (No. 242312), 2nd/5th Battalion Leicester Regiment, died on 26 September 1917 aged twenty. He was the son of William and Martha Ann Weston of Main Street. His death is recorded on the wall at Tyne Cot Cemetery and Memorial Passchendaele, Belgium.

Mary Ellen, Dorothy and Maud were the daughters of William and Martha Ann Weston. The dresses were made by Miss Julia Asher of Kilby for the Sunday School anniversary in 1916. The picture was taken for their brother, Sid, to carry with him during World War One.

The Cottage Homes Boys Band is pictured here in the ruins of Knaptoft Church, around 1910, where open-air services were held once a month during the summer.

Left: Alan Sydney Higgs (No. 14681681), Royal Leicester Regiment, was born on 15 July 1925 and died on 14 January 1998. The second son of Leivis and Nel Higgs (née Gillam) he enlisted at Warwick in November aged eighteen. He was wounded at Arnham in April 1945 and his right leg was amputated. He eventually recovered and returned to work at Tompkins' hosiery factory.

Above right: Jack Reginald Joyce (Able Seaman No. 334697) was a gunner who served on cruisers, destroyers and troopships. He was born at Blaby on 19 July 1912 and received the War Medal 1939-1945, the Atlantic Star (France and Germany bar), the African Star (North African bar 1942-1943) and the Italian Star. He died on 26 November 1998.

Flight Sergeant Robert Sidney Brothwell (No. 1238487) was in the RAF and trained pilots during The Second World War. He was killed in a training accident on 20 August 1943 when a trainee pilot crashed his plane.

Countesthorpe and Tur Langton Old Folks' Joy Day was held on 11 August 1931. The assembled people are waiting in The Square for the bus to take them to Tur Langton.

Ladies from Blaby, Countesthorpe and Narborough Mothers' Union outside St Andrew's Church, c. 1936. The group includes Lucy Edwards and her son John, Dolly Measures, the mother of Glyn and Keith, Phyllis Spence, Lou Riddington, Maud Riddington, Nellie Higgs, Sarah Hubbard, Frances Johnson.

The Service of Song, Earth's Fairest Robes, celebrating the centenary of the Baptist Sunday School in 1910. From left to right, back row: John Herbert, Thurston Root, Alfred Findley, Polly Findley, -?-, Roland Burley, Ewart Bowley. Third row: Elsie March, Olive Herbert, Lily Dalby, Maud Clowes, Eva Glazbrooke, Annie Clowes, Dorothy Herbert, Edith Yehm. Second row: Norah Bowley, -?-, Evelyn Chapman, May Morris, Nellie Chapman, Annie Chapman, Elsie Swann, -?-. Front row: -?-, -?-, -?-, Maggie Taylor, Edith Root, Dorothy Findley, -?-.

Eric and Vera Hewitt are pictured here at the first gate across the road from Countesthorpe to Peatling Magna. Children collected pennies from travellers for opening and closing the gate for them.

A Methodist wedding which took place on 25 May 1903. The following newspaper report echoes the feelings of Methodist villagers at the time: 'A very interesting wedding took place at Countesthorpe on Whit Monday. The contracting parties were Mr Fred Asher and Miss Emma Ward. Both belong to well known and highly respected families. The bridegroom's father has been a local preacher for thirty-five years, Society Steward for twenty-six years, a Sunday school teacher for forty years, and father and mother have been members of our church at Countesthorpe for forty-four years. The bride's father has been a Sunday school teacher for forty years; and the Ward family have been connected with our cause at Countesthorpe since its commencement, and their home has been the home of the ministers through all the years since. It was not surprising, therefore, that a marriage between two members of such well known families should be regarded as an important event, especially as the young people themselves are highly respected ... and have been members of the choir for over fifteen years.'

The wedding of Elsie March and Horace Riddington at Countesthorpe Baptist Church on 1 January 1914. The back row are, from left to right: Herbert Riddington (best man), Eliza Norton (bridesmaid), Mary Riddington, William Stephenson March (bride's father). Front row: Kathleen Gee, Horace Riddington, Elsie March, Edith Root (bridesmaid).

Dolly and John Snutch celebrated their golden wedding anniversary in 1997, the same year as the Queen and Prince Philip. They were invited to a party at Buckingham Palace on 15 July to celebrate the occasion. Dolly and John were married at St Andrew's Church on 5 April 1947.

A double wedding took place at St Andrew's Church on 22 May 1948. Ken Warner and his bride, Ellen Chapman, are on the left, and Ron Willis and his bride, Beryl Chapman, are on the right.

Two
Willoughby Waterleys

Posing for the camera in their car (the first in Willoughby Waterleys) are Miss Jenkyns, her friend, Revd Jenkyns and John Garratt, the chauffeur and gardener.

Mrs Annie Freer, née Wesson, standing outside her farmhouse, c. 1930. Until the 1930s the building on the right was a framework knitter's shop. The farmhouse has been demolished recently to make way for executive houses.

Caroline Taylor standing in the doorway of the cottage she shared with her mother, Rhoda Taylor. Caroline died in 1947 at the age of eighty-three.

John Goodman Illson, his father William
Illson and Ida Illson (who later became
Mrs Walter Heames) standing outside
their home during the early twentieth
century.

This village shop and post office was owned by the Thornicroft family but closed in 1983. Mrs
Frances Lavinia Frost, mother of Mrs Frances Thornicroft, is standing outside.

John Mawby and his wife, Emma. John was a carpenter, wheelwright and undertaker for fifty years. The carpenter's shop was once a Methodist chapel.

The school was built in 1846 with money that the late Samuel Simpson of Leicester and his sister, Elizabeth, left for charitable purposes. The highest number of children on roll was seventy, when additional children from Peatling Magna walked over the fields in good weather, and by road in winter, to attend the school. By 1964, however, the number of children had decreased to only eight and the school was closed down. Mrs Violet Shuttlewood was the last schoolmistress.

School children lined up across the street, 1908. The houses on the left, called Herberts Row, were built by the Herberts of Whetstone Pastures as accommodation for their employees. The three buildings in the centre were demolished to make an access for the council houses in Orchard Road. The General Elliott public house is on the far right. The earliest reference to the pub comes from 1810 when a sale of timber was to be held on the premises and the landlord was John Heath. In September 1810 William Taylor applied to the Quarter Sessions for the licence and in 1826 it was first mentioned by name in the Alehouse Recognisance Records. When the Alehouse Records first began in September 1753 there were four alehouses in the village. William Sharples, Robert Overton, Johnathan Brown and William Rippington applied for licences in that year, the largest number of applicants for a licence in one year until 1827.

Réné Garratt, her mother Ada Jane Garratt (née Tilley) and Roy (Ada's grandson) standing outside their home, Thistle Hall, around 1932. The Garratt family sold the house after the death of their father in 1964. It was deliberately burnt down and a modern house built on the site.

The parish church of St Mary as it appeared at the time when John Nichols was compiling his history of Leicestershire, *c.* 1794. (Leicestershire Record Office)

The interior of the church after it was restored by the Victorians, during the incumbency of the Revd Blucke. The beautiful oil lamps are of particular interest.

The rector, Revd Henry Strong Blucke, with village Sunday school children and their teachers in front of the rectory, *c.* 1898.

The church choir, *c.* 1908. Back row, left to right: -?-, -?-, Wilfred Hunt, -?-, Thomas Turrell, Mr J. Heames, John Garratt, -?-, -?-. Middle row: -?-, -?-, Florrie Heath (née Clark), Gertrude Frost, Miss Jenkyns, Revd J.L.H. Jenkyns, Elsie Hubbard, -?-, -?-, -?-. Front row: Martha Mawby, Clara Carr, Annie Turrell, Albert Carr, Connie Hubbard, -?-, Alice Campion (née Clark), Thomas James Turrell.

Main Street looking north, *c.* 1950. The cottage in the foreground was on the corner of Church Lane. Mrs Ann Carr was the last person to live there before it was demolished, soon after this photograph was taken. The wall behind it enclosed the rectory gardens. Across the road, the cottage in the centre was pulled down to give access to Orchard Close.

Manor Farm House, one of the earliest domestic brick buildings in Leicestershire. It was built in 1693, the date being scratched inconspicuously into a brick. It was the home of the Gamble family for over 100 years.

Clara Warden standing outside the house that had belonged to the Warden family since the early part of the eighteenth century. She died in the old family home on 26 July 1958 at the age of eighty-seven. After her death it was finally sold out of the family.

This Primitive Methodist Church was opened in 1877. The last wedding took place here on 1 March 1971. The marriage register dates from 1915 and is kept at the Leicestershire Record Office.

Jarvis Caleb Bennett outside his home early this century. He was a prominent member of the Methodist Church in the village. He and his wife, Matilda, had two daughters, Florence and Frances. He died on 26 November 1958 aged ninety-two.

One of a pair of two and a half storey houses in the village, the other being Nene House. The top storey would have contained bedrooms for the domestic servants. The present occupants are David Attfield and his wife. The little boy is Lional Buck and the date of the photograph is around 1930.

'The Limes' was another house built by Thomas Gamble in 1702. The pitched roof has finials on the gables. The brickwork is a chequer pattern of red and dark blue, and there is a walled garden that has gateposts with vases. In 1881 Thomas Bryan, and later his son Frank, farmed ninety-five acres of land.

Main Street looking north from the turning to Peatling Magna. The house in the right foreground was where the blacksmith, Jim Vincent, lived and worked. Behind the fence was a pond. The house has since been demolished and the pond filled in. Attfield's farmhouse is in the background.

The Old Hall, *c.* 1990. Pevsner describes this as a sixteenth- or early seventeenth-century timber house with projecting brick wings and a Georgian brick front. The initials 'R.G.' (Richard Gamble) and the date 1712 are incorporated into the brickwork on the south gable end.

An unknown family group poses for the camera outside the south front of The Old Hall, *c.* 1890. A branch of the Worthey family of Westend Farm moved into the property at the beginning of the twentieth century.

Hunts Lodge, on the bridle road from Willoughby to Gilmorton, *c.* 1913. Mrs Elizabeth Hunt is standing in the doorway and her son, Wilfred, with his wife, Mary, are in the centre. The village blacksmith, James Vincent, is on the right, holding his gun.

Members of another branch of the Worthey family posing for the camera outside West End Farm. They are, from left to right: William Worthey (a market gardener), his grandson Herbert, his wife Ann and his daughter Edith.

Standing in Turrell's orchard during 1935 are, from left to right: Mr and Mrs Ward, Frank Turrell, Kathleen Turrell, Mrs Turrell and Mr Thomas Turrell.

Annie Turrell was the daughter of Thomas James and Catherine Mary Turrell of Yew Tree Farm. She died on 8 November 1919, aged twenty-seven.

Sitting on the reaper, in about 1895, is
Mr Herbert Worthey of West End Farm,
with Mr Wesson and his son of Willoughby.

Members of the Wilkins family outside
Thistle Hall, c. 1900. The man standing on
the left is Ernest Warden.

Four Willoughby men photographed around the time of the First World War. Standing at the back are George Carr and Thomas Wilkins, and seated are Mr Dunkley and G. Illson.

This picture of Mary Wilkins (later Edwards) was taken during the First World War when she was a 'clippie' on the Leicester buses.

The shopkeeper is Frances Thornicroft. She is serving May Cooper (with the basket) and Lucy Vincent during the 1950s. The shop was also a post office and it closed down in 1983.

Jim and Lucy Vincent (née Gee) at an unidentified seaside resort, *c.* 1924. On his left is Lucy's half brother, Edwin Taylor and his wife, Mary Elizabeth (née Gillam).

The village cricket team in the yard of the General Elliott in 1906. The only two that have been identified are the two cricketers holding the bats. Wilf Hunt is on the left and Ernest Warden is on the right.

Villagers in fancy dress at the time of George VI's Coronation in 1937. These include Jinny Hubbard, Fred Hewitt, Fred Adley, Mary Warburton, Dorothy Oldershaw, Dody Freer, Herbert Freeson, Reg Stevens, Ken Vincent, Denis Freer, Peter Edwards, Peg Hill, Violet Heames, Bob Watson, David Watson, Billy Freer, George Worthey, Phyl Hunt, George Gee, Lilly Houghton, Doris Hill, Dorothy Heames.

Pupils from Willoughby School in 1933. On the back row are, from left to right: Wilfred Houghton, -?-, Derrick Houghton, Fred Porter, Douglas Edwin Hunt, Miss Mary Root. Middle row: Peter Edwards, Edith Evans, Eva Tanser, Violet Eames, Peggy Hill, Sid Tanser, Hilda Pegg, -?-, Barbara Houghton, Eddie Heath. Front row: -?-, -?-, -?-, Lional Buck, -?-, Denis Hill, -?-, Maurice Tanser.

A class of schoolchildren, c. 1928. On the back row are, from left to right: Olive Wright, James Absolam Reynolds, ? Reberdy, Ray Kind, Eddie Monk, Leonard Crutchley, Wilfred Kind, Mr Walter Perring, Charles Bannar, Edward Heath who died in World War Two, Leonard Heames, Wilfred Clarke, William Hill, Annie Goodwin, Rose Crutchley. Front row: Hilda Peg, Dorothy Kind, Phyllis Hunt, Gert Garratt, Millicent Thornicroft, Renie Porter, -?-, Eva Tanser, Mary Campion, Annie Houghton, Doris Hill, Dorothy Heames, Kittie Reynolds, Nancy Hill, Rennie Garratt, Chris Garratt, Sarah Houghton.

The wedding of Herbert Measures of Countesthorpe and Gertrude Ada Garratt took place on 9 September 1938 at the Primitive Methodist Church. The bride and groom can be seen here surrounded by many of their family and friends.

Reg Stevens and Phyllis Hunt were married on 29 April 1948 at St Mary's Church. They were married by Revd Winckley, the best man was Gregory Findley and Doreen Joblin was the matron of honour. The parents of the bride are Wilf and Mary Hunt.

Three
Peatling Magna

Manor Farm stands just east of All Saints Church, off Arnesby Lane. It is believed to have been built close to the site of the original manor house.

This postcard of Peatling Magna, taken around 1912, was the work of Miss Moore of Clarendon Park, Leicester. Hence the MCPL in the bottom right corner. The new village hall was opened in George V's Coronation year, 1911.

The eastern side of White House Farm, School Lane. The picture was taken on 10 May 1958. The farm has been the home of the Marshall family for many years.

This picture, taken around 1960, shows a section of the Countesthorpe to Peatling Magna road that was gated where the fields in the foreground were unhedged. The gate was positioned across the road in line with the first tree on the left. The haystacks, no longer a feature of the English countryside, are by the side of the road to Countesthorpe.

This is the view of the road looking towards Peatling Magna. It shows more clearly the fence to which the gate was attached and the unhedged fields of Peatling Magna parish. The road was gated to prevent cattle from straying onto neighbouring farmers' fields.

This row of cottages was demolished in the 1960s and was replaced by two modern detached houses. Brookhill Farmhouse remains little changed today, although it has lost its wooden portico.

PEATLING MAGNA.

These cottages on the edge of the village on the road to Countesthorpe are little changed today.

This picture of the village pub and Miss Jones' farmhouse was taken during the 1960s. Sid Barnett was the landlord of the pub at the time.

Vera Barnett, the landlady of the Cock Inn, chatting to a customer, *c.* 1973.

A more detailed view of the farmhouse and cottage next to the Cock Inn. The photograph was taken during the early 1970s, when the property was owned by Miss Jones.

Bruce Durno, the Huntsman, moving off after the meet at Peatling Magna, c. 1976. Colonel Murray Smith, the master of foxhounds, is on the right of the two following riders.

The eastern side of the All Saints parish church, *c.* 1900. It was originally built at the beginning of the twelfth century. The first vicar, Alan the chaplain, was noted in the Matriculous of Bishop Hugh of Lincoln in 1220. The spire was a fourteenth-century addition and some restoration also took place during this period. In 1729 the parish was united with Willoughby Waterleys, at the time when John Levett was the vicar. (Henton)

A postcard showing the northern side of All Saints Church, *c.* 1910.

The following church interiors are Henton photographs, taken around 1900. Of particular interest are the reredos and pulpit dated 1685 (note the sounding board over the pulpit), the screen (now situated under the tower) and the Royal Coat of Arms painted in wood. In 1906 a great deal of restoration work was completed under the vicar at that time, the Revd John L.H. Jenkyn.

The font is thirteenth-century, the font cover is seventeenth-century and the alabaster pillars were probably added in Victorian times. The benches seen in the nave have some early seventeenth-century carved ends with poppy-heads. At the time the church was lit with oil lamps.

Hall Farm, situated just across the road from Miss Jones' farmhouse. The photograph was taken during the early 1970s when the property was inhabited by Mr and Mrs Jones who was no relation to the aforementioned Miss Jones.

Pollards Farm on Main Street stood empty after the death of Miss Frances Ellen Pollard on 27 March 1965, aged eighty-two. She was the last member of the Pollard family who had been in the village since the beginning of the nineteenth century.

Local 'worthies' posing for the camera at the official opening of the village hall in 1911.

This picturesque village scene of a cobbled path and thatched cottages in School Lane creates a nostalgic image of Peatling Magna, *c.* 1900. Elizabeth Loomes, wife of Joseph Loomes, stands outside her cottage on the corner of Main Street and School Lane. All but two of their seven children were born in the village between 1852 and 1860. Elizabeth was the great grandmother of Albert and Gladys Clowes of Countesthorpe. She died in 1905, aged seventy-nine, and is buried in Peatling Magna churchyard.

Four

Foston

This postcard view, taken around 1906, shows what was possibly the last remaining house of the original Foston village. It survived until the 1930s on the Foston to Barlestone turnpike road. When the road was originally laid out, there was an inn in the vicinity. In 1750 the inn was mentioned in the will of Francis Cave. A further application for a licence was made in 1754 by John Cox, who was the grandson of William Cox, a member of the first generation of the Cox family to move to Foston.

The Spinney in the background stands on the site of the Manor House that was demolished around 1835. Hall Farm was built soon afterwards. Goodman Payne was the tenant farmer in 1841. The 1850 tithe map shows him farming 205 acres of land out of the 1,212 owned by Sir Charles Lamb, Lord of the Manor, in addition to 104 acres of rectorial glebe. His landlord was the rector, Revd John Henry Howlett. This photograph, taken in 1981, shows the sheep grazing the field known as the Walled Park.

Foston Lodge Farm (also known as Soar's Farm), shown here around 1922, was originally built as a farmworker's cottage. The people in the photograph are from the Barlow, Mawby and Page families of Countesthorpe.

As far as is known, no exterior picture of St Bartholomew's Church survives, but this interior view is of a painting completed before rebuilding in 1874. On the left is Faunt's tomb. Wall monuments to Revd John Lambert (1791) and his sister, Mrs Mary Harris (1807), still survive. The inscription of Faunt's tomb gives the following details: 'Here lieth the body of Henry Fawnt, esq. 2 sonne of Anthony Fawnt of Foston, esq. and Elizabeth his wife ... he died the 3 of May, 1665, in the 84 year of his age...'

This postcard, c. 1906, shows the parish church forty years after its restoration. Subscriptions raised for the restoration amounted to £815 9s 6d of which Sir Archibald Lamb, the Lord of the Manor, donated £150. The smallest amount given was one shilling.

St Bartholomew's decorated for Harvest Festival in the 1950s. Services were only held at Foston on one Sunday of every month. By this time there was no resident rector; the vicar of Countesthorpe was also the rector of Foston.

Communion 'Plate', given by Charles Boothby in 1781. It is stored in a bank vault and only brought out on very special occasions.

Revd Charles Wing, BA, Rector of Foston, was born on 13 September 1827 at Thornhaugh, Northamptonshire. He was the rector between 1868 and 1900. The 1871 census lists him with a wife, Elizabeth, born at Sedgebrook, Lincolnshire, and a son, George Staunton Wing, aged nine, born at Stanton-in-the-Vale, Nottinghamshire.

This picture of Foston Rectory was taken in 1983. The parish of Foston ceased to have a resident incumbent in the 1930s when the Revd H.J. Henry became the rector of Foston as well as the vicar of Countesthorpe. He lived at Countesthorpe Vicarage and so Foston Rectory became a private residence.

Sheep being driven to the Wednesday cattle market in Leicester, from Lodge Farm, Foston, down the old A50 Welford Road during the 1950s. Although the grazing of sheep was the reason for enclosure during the sixteenth century, the parish now has only arable farming.

Dr David Hoffler and his wife leaving Foston Church after the christening of their first child in 1975. The church is supported by a congregation of people made up from surrounding villages and towns.

Five
Kilby

The western approach to the village. This postcard of the Brook Bridge, *c.* 1930, creates a tranquil image. The brook flows into the River Sence at Kilby Bridge.

This second view, c. 1897, comes from a snapshot album, and shows the beginning of the path to the church, between the fence and the house. Near the church is an old hall-house, inhabited formerly by the St Johns.

Main Street, looking eastwards, c. 1906. The scene has changed little apart from an obvious increase in traffic.

The parish church of St Mary Magdalen stands away from the village across a field. It was rebuilt in 1858, replacing a small medieval church. The architecture was done by H. Goddard of Leicester. The replacement could seat 300 people.

This picture of Kilby Church's interior was taken in 1901 and shows the east window. The window was given as a memorial by the children of Revd Henry Kebble, the perpetual curate for fifty-four years between 1813 and 1867. The oak lectern shown was a memorial to Jonathan Glover. There is also a memorial window to Daniel Glover and, his wife, Sarah, and a brass memorial to Daniel, Jonathan and Joseph Glover. The church was renovated at a cost of £120 in memory of Queen Victoria.

The public elementary school on the right was erected in 1875 for eighty children. The average attendance in 1908, when Mrs Blanche Rawsthorne was Mistress, was fifty-five children. The field next to the school was owned by the Wells family who lived in the farmhouse opposite. Wells Avenue has now been built on the field, but it was previously the site for the fair that came to the village on 22 July.

The Dog and Gun public house on the left was run by William Chapman and his wife, Momento. They had one son and three daughters seen here in the picture. On the right is the post office run by Mrs Emily Aldgate. In recent years it was demolished to make way for the car park.

A view of Main Street looking east, showing houses on the north and south sides. The fourth doorway on the left led into Simons' shop. The building on the right-hand side of the road with the bay windows, and the adjoining building on its right, are part of the Dog and Gun public house. Next to that is Mr Porter's farmhouse while the gable-ended building on the right is Mr Lee's farmhouse. These smallholdings were County Council properties and were rented to encourage people back onto the land after World War One.

A picture of Main Street, Kilby, that was taken in 1906 looking west. In 1931 Mr Alf Smith kept the post office with his wife, Doris, in a cottage on the right-hand row. His wife also gave piano lessons. Mr Clarke, a carpenter and wheelwright, lived in the left-hand, white cottage.

The junction at Main Street, around 1905. The field road to Fleckney goes to the left, and the road to Wistow goes to the right.

Cottages on the field road to Fleckney at the junction with Main Street, *c.* 1905. The children and the woman posing for the camera make this a more saleable postcard.

An old house on the site of the original village of Kilby, situated on the north side of the church. The photograph was one of a series taken by Henton on 25 April 1906. The building still stands but is in desperate need of repair.

This picture of the Vicarage in Kilby comes from around 1908. The building has changed little in the last ninety years. It became a private house in the 1950s. The last incumbent to live at the vicarage was the Revd Eurich with his wife, Enid, and their five children. The vicarage is now called Glebe House and is occupied by the Millington family.

Kilby Lodge, a farmhouse, was in the occupation of Thomas F. Deacon in 1908, at the time when this photograph was taken in 1908. It stands outside the village, across the fields to the right of the road to Wistow.

This group of walkers, stretched across Kilby Lane, is making its way towards Wistow Park. At this point the River Sence runs parallel with the road.

This aerial view of Grange Farm, on the field road to Fleckney, was taken during the 1950s. The ridge and furrow in the foreground are the fossilized remains of medieval farming methods. The parish of Kilby was enclosed by an Act of Parliament in 1771.

Two men pose for an interesting picture of 1905 two-wheeled transport.

A couple in a pony and trap decorated for an event, perhaps the Coronation of 1911.

The Fernie Hunt meeting moving off from Kilby during March 1918. Mr C.W. Fernie's last year as Master. He died in 1919. The huntsman was Arthur Thatcher.

A car parked outside the old post office, c. 1925. The Black Swan public house is in the background.

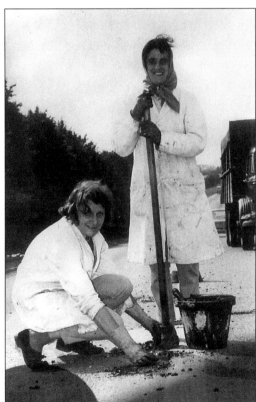

Joan and Ruth Chapman are seen here laying cats eyes – quite an unusual sight for the times! They were employed by Leicestershire County Council.

William Chapman, son of Henry and Jane Chapman of Countesthorpe, was born on 3 December 1857. William was the landlord of the Dog and Gun public house. He was also a smallholder, but started his working life as a bricklayer for his father.

Mr John Chapman was a labourer, who, like his daughters, worked for Leicestershire County Council. He was also a Special Constable.

This pair of pictures shows Charles Asher and his wife, Jane (née Gillam). Charles was born at Kilby, and was a grazier and carter.

Jane, the youngest daughter of John Gilliam and Mary Lord, was born in Countesthorpe. John was a framework knitter and poacher. He was shot and killed by the miller, George Keen, on 30 May 1868 at Crow Mill. He left a wife and nine children.

The teacher and pupils pose for a photograph at Kilby School, c. 1882. The teacher was Miss Lazenby and sitting on her knee is Alice Aldgate.

A school photograph from 1934. The back row are, from left to right: Greta Munton, Barbara Jeves, Joan Hallam, Sheila Swanwick, -?-, Ella Chapman, Joan Johnson, Richard Parker, Derick Wells, -?-. Middle row: Sheila Cramp, Sheila Ward, Sheila Parker, Ruth Chapman, Joyce Ellard, Betty Wooley, -?-. Front row, extreme left is David Cramp and next to him, John Swanwick. At the age of eleven, children went on to Wigston Magna (and Kibworth) if they passed the 11+ exam.

The May Queen and her attendants playing 'Devil Among the Taylors', a game of pub table skittles. Those present are, from left to right: May Mould (neé Wooley), Joan Piggin, Joan Gamble, (neé Johnson), Joyce Lee.

A group of Kilby scouts camping at Wistow. The scoutmaster at this time was George Brunskill.

Revd Ransome and the choirmaster seated with the Kilby Church Choir, c. 1928. The back row are, from left to right: Edgar Porter, -?-, -?-, Robert Watkins, Mr Sturman, -?-. On the extreme left, on her own, is Doris Lockett (née Asher) and the three boys intermingled in the centre are: Ron Bowers, -?- and Eric Gamble. Middle row: ? Watkins, Eileen Charlton, ? Watkins, Mary Looms, -?-, ? Watkins, Nora Bowe, Miss Madge Sturman, Mable Vann, Nora Bowers, -?-. Seated on the front row: Muriel, Grace Watkins, Lottie Wormleigh, Agnes Wormleigh, Mr Brunskill the choirmaster, Revd Ransome, Mrs Ransom, Mrs Edith Gamble. The two girls standing on the end are unknown.

The people standing at this Kilby wedding on 1 July 1910 are, from left to right: Alice Biggin (the daughter of Frank and Lucille), -?-, Frank Biggin, Frederick Gamble, Edgar Sutton, -?-, Lucilla Biggin (née Aldgate), Mrs Gamble (mother of the groom), Madge Biggin (daughter of Frank and Lucilla. Those sitting are: Mrs Emily Aldgate, Ethel Gamble, Edith Aldgate (the bride), Emily Ross, Gerty Taylor. Edith Aldgate, gained her teaching certificate at the age of twenty-three. She earned £1 6s 8d per month when she began teaching. This was raised to £20 per year after two years. She taught at Kilby School all her life, during which time she became headmistress.

102

Six
Newton Harcourt

The entrance to Newton Harcourt Manor House and gateHouse, taken during the early part of the twentieth century. This had been the home of the Goddard family since 1897, when Joseph Goddard, an architect, and his family moved from Leicester.

Mr and Mrs Henry Langton Goddard standing in front of their residence, with the tennis court in the foreground. The postcard was posted in February 1902.

The south side of the Manor House and garden showing the 'haha'. The 'haha' was a ditch and bank combination used to keep cattle out of gardens and parkland.

This view of the interior of Manor House was taken in the 1950s. It had remained unchanged for many years.

Postmarked November 1903 and sent to Australia, this postcard shows members of the Smart family outside their farmhouse on Specks Lane (now Post Office Lane).

These two pictures show village scenes during the 1950s. This row of cottages was originally built as four dwellings to house farm labourers and their families. They were built by the Cottesloes of Wistow Hall.

Newton Harcourt's only public house was situated in The Square. It closed in the 1880s and became an off licence. It has now closed down. The row of cottages at the rear housed farm labourers while the single-storey building on the right of the picture was the blacksmith's shop. The one on the left was a bakehouse.

John Asher Scotchbrook standing outside the Post Office.

The Scotchbrook family. Mary is on the left and her daughter, Emily, is on the right. Harry Scotchbrook, the father, is in the centre with Herbert, the youngest son, on his knee. Their other sons were Arthur, Harry, Leslie, William and Robert. Robert went to Canada but died in the First World War.

The founder members of the Newton Harcourt Women's Institute. The back row are, from left to right: Gladys May Bent, Mrs Potter or Shelton, Hilda Mott. Front row: Mrs Brooks, Louisa Scotchbrook, Nettie Bent, Mrs G. Wyatt.

This view of the Newton Harcourt Women's Institute in fancy dress was taken in 1927. Standing on the back row are, from left to right: Gladys Bent (née Grant), Midge Grant, Harriet Goddard, Mr Martin dressed as a woman, Oliver Reynolds, Frank Mott. The lady standing in between rows is Louisa Scotchbrook. Middle row: Miss Leavley, Hilda Mott (née Bradshaw), Mrs Haynes, Emily Scotchbrook, Annie Achuch, Hilda Reynolds (née Gardener), Edith Tyrrill, Daniel Goddard. Front row: Miss Craven (standing), Herbert Scotchbrook, Peggy Tyrrill, Dalice Fish, ? Gardener, Harry Tilley, Norman Tirrell, Nurse Martin, G.A. Wyatt.

This snapshot of St Luke's Church, c. 1895, shows the north side of the church and the entrance at the west end of the tower. The western tower contains one bell. The church, built in the Gothic style, was rebuilt in 1834 and seated 200.

This 1906 photograph of the church shows the simple 1834 interior with gas lighting and a pot-bellied heating stove added later. The register dates from around 1575. The silver plate, consisting of a chalice and cup, is Elizabethan.

On 1 August 1899 villagers from Newton Harcourt were out in force lining the route from the Manor House to St Luke's Church for the wedding of Margaret Jessica, the daughter of Joseph Goddard, to John Bartelot Aldridge.

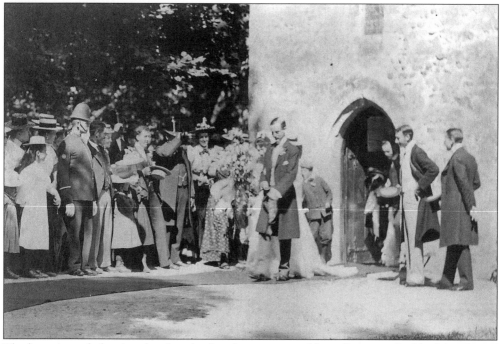

The happy couple leaving the church after the ceremony. Henry Langton Goddard, brother of the bride, is in the middle of the group of three men by the church door. The one policeman on duty for crowd control was paid ten shillings..

The wedding of Wilfred Herbert Lacey and Olive Brenda Woolley took place on 12 January 1935. The groom was a farm labourer from Stoughton and the bride was a domestic servant. The bride's father was Harry Woolley, the champion hedgecutter in the whole of England. The bride wore a white satin gown and carried a bouquet of Madonna lilies. The bridesmaids were Edith Slingsby, Betty Charlton, Betty Woolley and May Woolley. The best man was Mr A. Woolley. The wedding took place at St Luke's Church, perhaps the smallest church in Leicestershire. It was the first wedding held at the Newton Harcourt church for four years.

The wedding of David George Ingham and Gwen Wyatt was held on 27 April 1940. On the back row are, from left to right: Emily Goddard (née Scotchbrook), Harry Parris (Jnr), James Ingham, Cecil Black, Herbert Tilley, Harry Parris, Vera Black, Ethel Scotchbrook. Middle row: Alma Parris, Nancy Parris, Don Asher, Mabel Jordan, Alixei Jordan (the soldier), Louisa Scotchbrook (the best man), Joyce Powell (née Bent), Mary Parris, John Wyatt. Front row: George Ellingworth (standing), Elizabeth Ingham (née Jones), Annie Maria Scotchbrook (née Asher), David George Ingham, Gwen Wyatt, Ann Wyatt, G.A. Wyatt, Pauline O'Sullivan (née Black).

A stretch of the Grand Union Canal taken from Bridge 80 on the Newton Harcourt road.

This picture, taken during the late 1890s, shows Joseph Goddard sitting at the front of the wagonette with Miss Blanche Eastwood. Mrs Annie Goddard is sitting behind with two of their grandchildren.

Mrs Gertrude Goddard, the wife of Henry Langton Goddard, seated in her horse and trap.

Henry Langton Goddard with his wife, Gertrude, and the gardener, Thompson. This is one of a set of five photographs taken by Stretton, photographers from Fleckney.

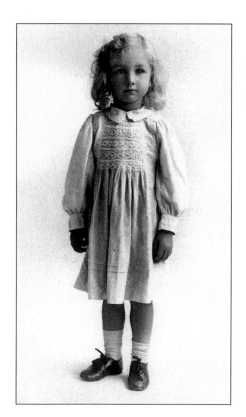

Henry Langton Goddard during his childhood. Little boys often wore dresses until they were four or five years old, when they were put into knickerbockers and had their hair cut. This custom was discontinued after the First World War.

Miss Amy Oliver, who later became Mrs Joseph Faulkner of Locke House, Newton Harcourt. She was nanny to Henry Langton Goddard.

114

Henry Langton Goddard was an officer in the Leicestershire Regiment during the First World War.

Major John Bartelot Aldridge (DSO, RHA, Rocket Troop), was one of the sons-in-law of Joseph Goddard. He died in a polo accident at Simla, India, c. 1908.

The first district nurse of Newton Harcourt, Wistow and Kilby. Her name is unknown.

Miss Louisa Scotchbrook was the post lady for many years. Her family ran the post office.

Mr Wyatt travelling on the road between Newton Harcourt and Wistow. The two magnificent elm trees, once a common feature of the English countryside, have now been lost to Dutch Elm Disease.

Herbert Tilley clearing up the garden. Note the carpets on the line, ready for beating.

Joseph Waterton was the gamekeeper at Wistow and later became the keeper and woodman at Newton Harcourt. He died around 1970.

Mrs Gwen Ingham is seen here behind the counter of the village shop and post office during the mid-1950s.

This picture of schoolchildren from Newton Harcourt and Wistow was taken in the middle of the 1890s. The only child that can be identified is Mary Scotchbrook who is on the far right of the back row.

Children from Newton Harcourt School with their teacher who may have been a Miss Hedges. The children standing on the back row are, from left to right: ? Jones, Peggy Tirrell, Horace Jones, Harry Tilley, Bert Sheppard, ? Edwards, Emily Sheppard, ? Edwards, Leslie Gardener. Seated on the front row: Joyce Bent, Ivy Sheppard, John Dodson, Gwen Wyatt, John Gardener, Katie Jones, Mildred Jones, -?-, Nancy Dodson.

Village school children dancing round the maypole during the early 1950s. They include Joyce Bent, Ivy Sheppard, John Dodson, Gwen Wyatt, John Gardener, Katie Jones, Mildred Jones, Nancy Dodson.

Henry Langton Goddard accompanied by a large number of family, friends and villagers in June 1911. Included in this group are Mrs Smart, Vera Heywood, Revd Ransome, Mr and Mrs Freckleton, Mrs Emma Scotchbrook, Louisa and Leslie Scotchbrook, Edgar Smart, Herbert Tilley and his wife.

Seven

Wistow

A view, taken during the 1890s, of the north side of St Wistan's Church. There are many old tombstones in the churchyard, but none are more recent than 1873 when burials ceased because of the danger of floods.

These two postcards show scenes of Wistow which have changed little in the last ninety years. The one above shows the road running past the lake. The one below shows the road and lake with Wistow Hall in the background. In 1814 Wistow was inherited by Dr Henry Vaughan who had changed his name to Halford by an Act of Parliament five years earlier, in anticipation of this inheritance. Sir Henry Halford made extensive improvements to the property of Wistow and created a lake in the grounds, diverting the road round it at the same time.

The south-west corner of Wistow Hall, *c.* 1904. During the First World War, the Hall was made available as a hospital for wounded soldiers by Lord and Lady Cottesloe. Between 1914 and 1919 there were 440 British patients, 16 Belgians and 4 Canadians. During the Second World War, Wistow was initially a home for babies bombed-out by the Blitz, and later became the home for a number of expatriate Lutheran priests.

The south front of Wistow Hall, *c.* 1904. King Charles I slept at Wistow on 4 June 1645, prior to the Battle of Naseby. During their flight from the battlefield, the King and Prince Rupert were given fresh horses at Wistow, leaving behind their own elaborate saddles.

This view of Wistow Hall is taken from Fleckney Road. The cattle are grazing on what was probably the site of Wistow village.

A view of the west front of Wistow Hall, taken around 1930. Note the glasshouses, used for growing exotic fruits, such as peaches and nectarines.

Skating on the lake at Wistow, *c.* 1908.

William Woolley, known locally as 'Bill', was the farm foreman at Wistow Estate for many years. In his younger days he was an expert hedgecutter and won the open hedgecutting championships in Leicestershire four times in succession. He was still at work on 24 October 1942 when he died at the age of seventy-nine.

Arthur Woolley of Wistow hedging on the Great Glen Road at Newton Harcourt.

The wedding of Arthur Henry Woolley and Gladys Irene Dixon took place on 16 July 1938. The bridegroom was a farmer at Wistow Lodge Farm and the bride was a domestic servant. This was the first wedding for over five years at St Wiston Church. The bride wore a white satin gown and carried a bouquet of pink carnations. The bridesmaids were Miss May Woolley and Miss Annie Heggington. The best man was Mr W. Lacey.

The majority of these football players would probably have been estate workers from Wistow Hall or come from local farms.

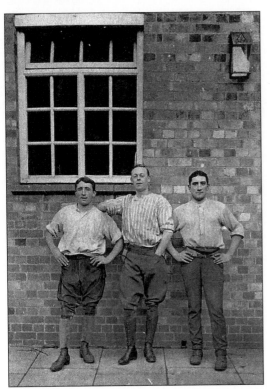

Three grooms from Wistow Hall. The stud groom in 1908 was Samuel Peat.

Two cyclists riding through Wistow Park towards Kilby.